LE CORDON BLEU

HOME COLLECTION

·SAUCES·

PERIPLUS
EDITIONS

contents

recipe ratings ☸ easy ☸☸ a little more care needed ☸☸☸ more care needed

White wine sauce

This elegant sauce is shown here with poached white fish and vegetables.

Preparation time **10 minutes**
Total cooking time **40 minutes**
Makes approximately 1¹/4 *cups*

I tablespoon unsalted butter
3 shallots, finely chopped
I¹/4 cups white wine
I¹/4 cups chicken or fish stock (see page 61)
I³/4 cups heavy cream

1 Melt the butter in a heavy-bottomed saucepan over low heat. Gently cook the shallots in the saucepan, without coloring, until they are soft and transparent.

2 Pour in the white wine, scraping the base of the saucepan with a wooden spoon. Turn up the heat and boil until the liquid has reduced by half. Add the stock and boil until the liquid has reduced to ¹/3 cup.

3 Stir in the cream and continue to reduce the sauce until it is thick enough to coat the back of a spoon.

4 Pass the sauce through a fine strainer if you wish. Season, to taste, with salt and pepper. Serve warm. It may be kept warm in the top of a double boiler over barely simmering water for up to half an hour before serving. Do not allow the water to boil at this stage or the sauce may separate. This sauce goes best with fish or chicken.

Chef's tips Use a stock to complement the dish with which you serve it, for example, a chicken stock for chicken dishes.

To prevent a skin from forming on the sauce while keeping hot, cover the surface directly with plastic wrap.

Green peppercorn sauce

This pungent peppery sauce, laced with brandy, is pictured with steak and new potatoes.

Preparation time **10 minutes**
Total cooking time **15 minutes**
Makes approximately ³/4 *cup*

2 tablespoons drained green peppercorns
¹/3 cup brandy
I¹/4 cups brown or lamb stock (see page 60)
¹/3 cup heavy cream

1 Place the peppercorns in a heavy-bottomed saucepan and, at a very low heat, warm through for 1–2 minutes, until dry, being careful not to burn them. Coarsely break the peppercorns against the sides of the saucepan using the back of a wooden spoon.

2 Pour the brandy into the saucepan, turn up the heat and quickly boil for 1–2 minutes, or until the brandy has evaporated. Stir in the stock, bring to a boil and boil for about 5 minutes, or until the liquid has reduced by one quarter.

3 Add the cream and continue to reduce over high heat until the sauce coats the back of the spoon. Season, to taste, with salt, and pepper if required. Serve immediately, with juicy broiled or pan-fried red meat such as steak or chops.

Chef's tip This sauce has quite a strong peppery taste because the green peppercorns are cooked in the sauce from the beginning. If you want instead a burst of flavor from each individual peppercorn, proceed with steps 1 and 2 up to evaporating the brandy. In a separate saucepan, reduce the stock and cream, then add to the peppercorns and brandy. Stir and season to taste.

White wine sauce (top) and Green peppercorn sauce

Creamy mushroom sauce

Button mushrooms lend a mild, earthy flavor to this sauce, which we have shown with char-grilled filet mignon, steamed baby zucchini and carrots.

*Preparation time **15 minutes***
*Total cooking time **15 minutes***
*Makes approximately **1¹/2 cups***

❁

1/4 cup unsalted butter
4 large shallots, finely chopped
2¹/4 cups finely chopped button mushrooms
leaves from 1 stem of fresh tarragon
1/3 cup white wine
2¹/3 cups brown stock (see page 60)
2 tablespoons whipping cream or sour cream

1 Melt the butter over low heat in a skillet. Add the shallots and cook for 2 minutes, or until soft and transparent, without coloring. Increase the heat, add the mushrooms and tarragon and cook for 5–7 minutes, or until the mushrooms are golden brown. The mushrooms will make their own liquid. Cook until this has evaporated and they are dry.
2 Pour in the white wine, scraping the bottom of the pan with a wooden spoon to lift off the sticky sediment that contains a lot of flavor. Add the stock and boil until it has reduced by half. Season, to taste, with salt and pepper. Strain and transfer the mushrooms to a food processor or blender and blend until smooth. Add the stock, a couple of tablespoons at a time, then add the cream and blend to combine. Transfer to a saucepan to reheat as necessary. To serve, pour the sauce into a warmed sauce boat, pour onto the base of a plate and serve the food on top or pour over the food. Serve with broiled or barbecued meat or poached white fish or chicken.

Mustard sauce

This is a smooth, piquant sauce perfect to serve with rabbit, veal or pork. We have shown it with roast veal and potatoes.

*Preparation time **10 minutes***
*Total cooking time **20 minutes***
*Makes approximately **1 cup***

❁

1 tablespoon unsalted butter
1 large shallot, finely chopped
1/3 cup white wine
1¹/4 cups brown stock (see page 60)
3 tablespoons heavy cream
2 tablespoons Dijon mustard

1 Melt the butter in a saucepan over low heat, add the shallot and cook gently, without coloring, until soft and transparent.
2 Pour in the wine, scraping the base of the saucepan with a wooden spoon to lift and blend in the flavorful sediment. Stir in the stock, bring to a boil and then reduce the heat to a simmer. Boil, uncovered, until the liquid has reduced by half. Stir in the cream, simmer for another 2–3 minutes and then strain the sauce through a fine strainer into a clean saucepan.
3 Whisk in the Dijon mustard and season, to taste, with salt and pepper. Reheat gently to serve.

White sauce

Create a variety of sauces by adding flavors to this basic sauce, pictured here with broccoli and cauliflower. See page 62 for step-by-step instructions to accompany this recipe.

Preparation time **5 minutes**
Total cooking time **10 minutes**
Makes approximately 2¹/4 cups

❂

2 tablespoons unsalted butter
¹/4 cup all-purpose flour
2 cups milk
small pinch of ground nutmeg

1 Melt the butter in a heavy-bottomed saucepan over medium-low heat. Sprinkle the flour over the butter and cook for 1–2 minutes without allowing it to color, stirring constantly with a wooden spoon.
2 Remove the saucepan from the heat and slowly add the milk, whisking to avoid lumps. Return to medium heat and bring to a boil, stirring constantly. Cook for 3–4 minutes, or until the sauce coats the back of a spoon. If the sauce has lumps, pass it through a fine strainer and reheat in a clean saucepan. Season with salt, pepper and nutmeg. Serve hot.

Chef's tip Flavor the sauce by adding an onion studded with cloves to the milk, then warming the milk through.

Mornay sauce

A white sauce enriched with cheese and egg yolks makes a perfect topping for the scallops shown here. To finish, simply flash under the broiler until golden brown.

Preparation time **10 minutes**
Total cooking time **15 minutes**
Makes approximately 2¹/4 cups

❂

2 tablespoons unsalted butter
¹/4 cup all-purpose flour
2 cups milk
2 egg yolks
³/4 cup shredded Gruyère cheese
pinch of ground nutmeg

1 Melt the butter in a heavy-bottomed saucepan over medium-low heat. Sprinkle the flour over the butter and cook for 1–2 minutes without allowing it to color, stirring constantly with a wooden spoon.
2 Remove the saucepan from the heat and slowly add the milk, whisking to avoid lumps. Return to medium heat and bring to a boil, stirring constantly. Cook for 3–4 minutes, or until the sauce coats the back of a spoon. If the sauce has lumps, pass it through a fine strainer and reheat in a clean saucepan.
3 Remove from the stove, add the yolks and cheese off the heat and mix. Season with salt, pepper and nutmeg.

White sauce (top) and Mornay sauce

Suprême sauce

This creamy velouté sauce is the accompaniment to the classic poached chicken dish, Chicken suprême. It is also delicious, however, with broiled chicken breast as shown here.

Preparation time **5 minutes**
Total cooking time **15 minutes**
Makes approximately **3¹/4 cups**

3 tablespoons unsalted butter
¹/3 cup all-purpose flour
1³/4 cups hot chicken stock (see page 61)
1¹/2 cups heavy cream
3 tablespoons unsalted butter, cut up, optional

1 Melt the butter in a deep heavy-bottomed saucepan over medium-low heat. Sprinkle the flour over the butter and cook for 1–2 minutes without allowing it to color, stirring constantly with a wooden spoon. The mixture should be white and frothy. Remove from the heat. Stir in a little hot stock and blend well using a wooden spoon or whisk. Little by little, add the remaining stock.

2 Return to the heat and whisk to avoid lumps as you slowly bring the sauce to a boil. Lower the heat and gently simmer for 3–4 minutes, stirring or whisking constantly. Stir in the cream and continue to simmer for 2–3 minutes, or until the sauce coats the back of a spoon. If the sauce has lumps, pass it through a fine strainer and reheat in a clean saucepan. Season with salt and white pepper. To add extra shine, whisk in the butter pieces. Serve this sauce immediately.

Caper sauce

Traditionally served with boiled leg of lamb, this sauce with its sharp, piquant taste of capers is also excellent with lamb loin roast and vegetables as shown.

Preparation time **15 minutes**
Total cooking time **45 minutes**
Makes approximately **2 cups**

2 tablespoons unsalted butter
¹/4 cup all-purpose flour
2 cups hot lamb stock (see page 60)
2 egg yolks
3 tablespoons heavy cream
3 tablespoons drained capers, chopped

1 Melt the butter in a medium-size, deep heavy-bottomed saucepan over medium-low heat. Sprinkle the flour over the butter, mix in and cook gently, stirring constantly, until the mixture is light golden. Remove from the heat.

2 Stir in a little hot stock and blend well using a wooden spoon or whisk. Return to the heat and whisk to avoid lumps as you slowly bring the sauce to a boil. Little by little, add the remaining stock. Reduce the heat and cook gently for another 30 minutes, stirring occasionally. Check that the sauce coats the back of the spoon before straining into a clean saucepan. If too thick, add a little more stock. If too thin, cook a little longer to reduce the sauce.

3 In a bowl, mix the egg yolks and cream. Stir in a little of the strained sauce, combine thoroughly and pour back into the saucepan. Stir to combine and warm gently to thicken the yolks. Do not boil. The sauce will separate if it overheats. Add the capers and season to taste. Serve immediately with lamb.

Suprême sauce (top) and Caper sauce

Beurre fondu

This classic sauce can be varied by the liquid used to suit the dish with which it is served. It can be served with vegetables, chicken or fish. We have pictured it with a selection of vegetables.

Preparation time **5–7** *minutes*
Total cooking time **10** *minutes*
Makes approximately 1 cup

❁

3 tablespoons water, dry white wine or chicken stock (see page 61)
3/4 cup unsalted butter, cut into small cubes and chilled
lemon juice, to taste

1 Place the liquid (water, dry white wine or chicken stock) into a small saucepan and bring to a boil.
2 While the liquid is simmering, use a whisk or an electric mixer to beat in the cubes of butter, a few at a time, to obtain a smooth consistency. Remove the saucepan from the heat and season to taste with some lemon juice, salt and pepper. Serve the sauce immediately, or keep it warm (not hot), covered with plastic wrap, in the top of a double boiler over warm water, for up to 30 minutes before use.

Chef's tip If the sauce becomes too cold, it will set. Warm it by stirring over a saucepan of hot water. If it becomes too hot, it will separate. Remove the insert from the water and stir in a chip of ice or a few drops of cold water.

Beurre blanc

Another exquisite classic, seasoned with shallots, which is ideal to serve with fish such as the poached salmon steak shown in the picture.

Preparation time **10** *minutes*
Total cooking time **25** *minutes*
Makes approximately 1 cup

❁

2 large shallots, very finely chopped
1/3 cup white wine vinegar
1/3 cup dry white wine
3/4 cup unsalted butter, cut into small cubes and chilled

1 Add the shallots, white wine vinegar and white wine to a small wide-bottomed saucepan and heat over medium heat until the liquid has evaporated to 2 tablespoons.
2 As soon as the liquid boils, reduce the heat to very low and whisk in the butter, piece by piece. Whisk constantly to achieve a smooth and pale sauce. Season to taste with salt and pepper. Serve immediately, or transfer the sauce to the top of a double boiler, cover with plastic wrap and place over warm water until ready to serve. You may wish to strain the sauce for a smoother consistency. Serve with fish or chicken dishes.

Chef's tip Try adding a pinch of saffron threads with the wine. Also, try adding finely grated orange, lime or lemon rind or a small amount of chopped herbs such as tarragon, chives or dill weed.

Beurre fondu (top) and Beurre blanc

Mousseline sauce

An easy but delicious sauce, shown here with steamed beans and poached white fish fillet.

Preparation time **15 minutes**
Total cooking time **5 minutes**
Makes approximately **2 cups**

3/4 cup clarified butter (see page 63)
3 egg yolks
small pinch of cayenne pepper, to taste
juice of 1/2 lemon
2 tablespoons whipping cream

1 Melt the butter in a small saucepan. Place the egg yolks and ¼ cup water in the top of a double boiler and whisk until foamy. Place the insert over barely simmering water and continue to whisk until thick and the mixture leaves a trail on the surface when the whisk is lifted.

2 Remove the insert from the water and gradually add the melted butter, whisking constantly. When all the butter is incorporated, season with cayenne pepper, lemon juice and salt. Keep the sauce warm over the saucepan of warm water off the heat.

3 Beat the cream until the trail made by the whisk or beaters can be seen, but if the bowl is tilted the cream just runs thickly. Fold the cream lightly into the sauce. This sauce is excellent with poached fish or asparagus. Mousseline sauce is always served warm.

Chef's tip At no time must this sauce be allowed to get too hot or the yolks will cook and separate from the butter. To remedy, remove the insert from the water and try adding a few drops of cold water or a chip of ice and whisking vigorously.

Béarnaise sauce

This creamy, tangy sauce is pictured with filet mignon, potatoes and baby cauliflower.

Preparation time **20 minutes**
Total cooking time **10 minutes**
Makes approximately **1 1/2 cups**

1 cup clarified butter (see page 63)
2 tablespoons fresh tarragon, coarsely chopped
2 tablespoons fresh chervil, coarsely chopped
1 shallot, finely chopped
4 peppercorns, crushed coarsely under a heavy saucepan
1/3 cup white wine vinegar
6 egg yolks
pinch of cayenne pepper

1 Melt the butter in a small saucepan. Set aside 1 tablespoon tarragon and 1/2 tablespoon chervil. Place the shallot and peppercorns in a separate small saucepan with the vinegar and remaining tarragon and chervil. Bring to a boil and simmer for 4–6 minutes, or until the liquid has reduced by three quarters.

2 Transfer the liquid to the top of a double boiler over barely simmering water. Add the egg yolks and whisk until thick and the mixture leaves a trail on the surface when the whisk is lifted.

3 Remove the insert from the water and gradually pour in the butter, whisking constantly, until all the butter in incorporated. Strain, then season with salt and cayenne pepper. Add the reserved tarragon and chervil just before serving. Serve lukewarm, don't overheat. If the sauce separates, whisk in a few drops of cold water or chips of ice to restore consistency. The sauce may be kept warm, covered with plastic wrap, over the saucepan of warm water.

Hollandaise sauce

This smooth, butter-based basic sauce is famed for serving with asparagus, as shown. See page 63 for step-by-step instructions to accompany this recipe.

*Preparation time **10 minutes***
*Total cooking time **10 minutes***
Makes approximately 2 cups

3/4 cup clarified butter (see page 63)
3 egg yolks, at room temperature
pinch of cayenne pepper (see Chef's tips)
1 teaspoon lemon juice

1 Melt the butter in a small saucepan. Place the egg yolks and ¼ cup water in the top of a double boiler and whisk until foamy. Place over barely simmering water and continue whisking until thick and the mixture leaves a trail on the surface when the whisk is lifted.
2 Gradually add the butter, whisking constantly. When all the butter is incorporated, strain the sauce into a sauce boat and season with salt to taste, cayenne pepper and lemon juice. Serve immediately. Keep the sauce warm by leaving the sauce in the insert and covering the surface directly with plastic wrap. Place the insert over the pan of warm water.

Chef's tips If the sauce becomes too cold, it will set. Warm it by increasing the heat under the pan of hot water. If it becomes too hot, it will separate. Remove the insert from the water and stir in a chip of ice or a few drops of cold water.

Measure out small amounts of cayenne pepper using the tip of a knife. Avoid using your fingertips as the residual pepper can cause discomfort if accidentally rubbed into the eyes or onto the lips.

Tomato sauce

This excellent tomato sauce, full of flavor, is shown here with deep-fried battered fish, but it would also be delicious served with burgers or pasta.

*Preparation time **20 minutes***
*Total cooking time **45 minutes***
Makes approximately 1³/4 cups

12 very ripe tomatoes or 4 x 16 oz. cans tomatoes, drained and coarsely chopped
3 tablespoons olive oil
2 tablespoons tomato paste
2/3 cup diced carrots
2/3 cup diced onions
2/3 cup diced bacon
4 sprigs of fresh thyme
2 bay leaves
small pinch of cayenne pepper

1 If using fresh tomatoes, score a small cross in the bases, put in a bowl and cover with boiling water. Allow to stand for 10 seconds before plunging them into a bowl of iced water. Drain and, with the point of a sharp knife, remove the stalk and then peel, quarter and remove the seeds. Coarsely chop the flesh.

2 Heat the olive oil in a saucepan over medium heat. Stir the tomato paste into the oil and cook for 30 seconds, stirring constantly with a wooden spoon to avoid burning. Stir in the carrots, onions and bacon and continue to cook gently, without coloring, for another 10 minutes, or until the vegetables are tender.

3 Add the tomatoes, thyme and bay leaves to the pan and gently cook for 30 minutes (longer if using canned tomatoes), stirring occasionally. Strain through a coarse strainer, pressing with a wooden spoon to extract as much liquid and pulp as possible. Discard the ingredients in the strainer. Season with salt and cayenne pepper and serve hot.

Apple sauce

The tartness of this sauce is the perfect accompaniment to roast pork, as pictured, and also for more fatty meats, such as duck or goose.

*Preparation time **15 minutes***
*Total cooking time **15 minutes***
Makes approximately 2 cups

4 medium-large tart cooking apples, peeled and cut into small cubes
pinch of cinnamon or cumin
2 teaspoons sugar

1 Combine the apple cubes, cinnamon or cumin and sugar in a saucepan and add enough water to barely cover the base of the pan. Cover with waxed paper and a lid and cook the apples over low-medium heat for 10–15 minutes, or until the apples have broken down to a purée. You may need to mash the apples with a fork or push it through a strainer to remove any lumps.

2 If a runnier consistency is required, add some water towards the end of cooking. Also, you may adjust the sweetness with more sugar to taste. Serve hot or cold.

3 To make in the microwave, place the apples in a large microwave-safe dish with the cinnamon or cumin and sugar. Microwave on High for about 4 minutes, or until the apples break down to a purée when pressed against the side of the dish with a fork.

Tomato coulis

A fresh tomato sauce that requires no cooking is perfect served in summer with char-grilled vegetables, such as the zucchini, eggplant and bell peppers pictured, or savory mousses.

Preparation time **20 minutes**
Total cooking time **None**
Makes approximately **2²/3 cups**

6 very ripe tomatoes
1 large shallot, chopped
2 teaspoons olive oil
1 tablespoon balsamic vinegar
2 tablespoons tomato paste, optional

1 Bring a saucepan of water to a boil. Meanwhile, cut a small cross in the bases of the tomatoes. Put them in a bowl, cover with boiling water and let stand for 10 seconds before plunging them into a bowl of iced water. Drain and, with the point of a sharp knife, remove the stalk and then peel, quarter and remove the seeds. Coarsely chop the flesh.

2 Blend the tomatoes and shallot in a blender until smooth. Pass them through a fine strainer and transfer to a round-bottomed bowl.

3 Set the bowl on a towel to prevent it from moving while whisking. Gradually add the oil, in a thin steady stream, while whisking constantly. Once the mixture has emulsified or thickened, add the balsamic vinegar and season with salt and pepper. Alternatively, return the strained tomato mixture to the blender and add the oil and vinegar as above. If the sauce does not have a shiny red color or the tomato taste is very weak, whisk in the tomato paste to enhance both the color and the taste.

Chef's tip When tomatoes are not in season, drained canned tomatoes could be used instead of fresh.

Red pepper coulis

Use this coulis in the same way as a tomato coulis when a different flavor is required. It is shown here with broiled chicken kebabs.

Preparation time **10 minutes**
Total cooking time **25 minutes**
Makes approximately **3/4 cup**

3 red bell peppers
1 tablespoon unsalted butter or olive oil
2 shallots, finely chopped
1 clove garlic, finely chopped
1 cup chicken or brown veal stock
  (see pages 60–61)

1 Cut the bell peppers in half, remove the seeds and membrane, press the peppers flat and lightly oil the skins. Cook under a preheated broiler, skin-side-up, until the skin is evenly blistered and blackened. Remove, place in a plastic bag and when cool, peel away the skin and chop the flesh into evenly sized pieces.

2 Heat the butter or oil in a heavy-bottomed saucepan, add the shallots and garlic and cook gently for 1–2 minutes, without coloring, until softened. Add the bell peppers, pour in 3/4 cup of the stock and bring to a boil. Reduce the heat and simmer for about 10 minutes until the liquid has reduced by half. Mash the soft peppers against the sides of the pan to make a thick purée or purée in a blender or food processor until smooth. Season to taste with salt and pepper.

3 Pass through a strainer and adjust the consistency with the remaining stock, if necessary. The coulis should coat the back of a spoon. Serve warm or chilled.

Chef's tip Use a stock to complement the dish it is intended to accompany, such as a fish stock for fish dishes, vegetable stock for vegetable dishes.

Tomato coulis (top) and Red pepper coulis

Bread sauce

A classic accompaniment to roast chicken, turkey or game, this delicately flavored sauce is a favorite of the English. It is shown here with turkey and vegetables.

*Preparation time **5 minutes + 15 minutes standing***
*Total cooking time **15 minutes***
Makes approximately 1 cup

1³/4 cups milk
1 small onion or 2 large shallots
8 whole cloves
2 bay leaves
1¹/2 cups fresh white bread crumbs

1 Pour the milk into a saucepan and place over medium heat. Stud the onion or shallots with the cloves and add to the milk with the bay leaves. Bring slowly to a boil. Remove from the heat, cover and set aside for 15 minutes to allow the flavors to infuse into the milk.
2 Strain the milk through a fine strainer and discard the flavoring ingredients. Gradually add the bread crumbs, whisking constantly, until the sauce has thickened to a thick pouring consistency. Season to taste with salt and pepper.
3 The sauce may be made a day in advance, although some additional milk should be added when reheating because the bread crumbs will have absorbed more milk overnight. Serve the sauce warm from a sauce boat.

Chef's tip You can also add a pinch of nutmeg or infuse the milk with other flavors such as peppercorns. Stir in a few raisins if serving the sauce with game. Stir in a little cream or a tablespoon of butter at the end for a richer sauce.

Rouille

This is the delicious traditional accompaniment for the bouillabaisse shown here.

*Preparation time **20 minutes***
*Total cooking time **1 hour 20 minutes***
Makes approximately 1¹/4 cups

1 medium baking potato
1 red bell pepper
1 egg yolk
1 teaspoon tomato paste
1 clove garlic, peeled
¹/2 cup olive oil
pinch of cayenne

1 Preheat the oven to 350°F. Place the potato on a baking sheet and pierce it several times with a fork. Bake for 1 hour, or until tender when tested with the point of a small knife. Alternatively, pierce the potato all over, wrap in a paper towel and microwave on High for 4–6 minutes, turning halfway through cooking. When cool enough to handle, cut in half and scoop out the flesh into a food processor.
2 Cut the bell pepper in half and remove the seeds and membrane. Lightly oil the skin and cook under a preheated broiler, skin-side-up, until the skin is blistered and blackened. Alternatively, bake for 15 minutes. Place in a plastic bag and when cool, peel away the skin. Add the flesh to the food processor with the egg yolk, tomato paste and garlic. Blend until smooth.
3 While the machine is running, gradually pour in the oil in a thin steady stream, until well incorporated. Season to taste with salt, pepper and cayenne pepper, remembering that the rouille should be quite fiery. Serve in a bowl or spread onto crisp bread croûtes. If serving as an accompaniment to a bouillabaisse, place a spoonful in the center of each serving.

Pesto

This classic, uncooked basil, Parmesan and pine nut sauce is traditionally served with pasta, as pictured.

*Preparation time **15 minutes***
*Total cooking time **None***
Makes approximately 3¹/4 cups

❋

1³/4 cups firmly packed fresh basil leaves
1 cup shredded Parmesan
2 cloves garlic, peeled
¹/3 cup pine nuts (pignoli)
¹/3 cup olive oil

1 Wash the basil leaves well and dry thoroughly in a salad spinner or gently pat dry using a paper towel.
2 Process the Parmesan in a food processor until it resembles fine bread crumbs. Add the garlic and pine nuts (pignoli) and process briefly to coarsely combine the ingredients. Add the basil at this point and process to combine.
3 While the machine is still running, slowly add the olive oil until a paste is formed. Season to taste with salt and pepper, then continue to add the oil until it reaches a spoonable consistency. Serve the pesto stirred into spaghetti or with char-grilled vegetables or meats. To store, cover and refrigerate for up to 3 days.

Chef's tip If you wish to store the pesto for a longer period, transfer it to a sterilized jar, cover the surface with olive oil and store the jar in the refrigerator. Once opened, the pesto must be used within 2–3 days.

Tomato concassée

This is a classic vegetable preparation. "Concassée" is also used to describe finely diced tomato used as a garnish. It is shown here with ravioli.

*Preparation time **15 minutes***
*Total cooking time **15 minutes***
Makes approximately 1 cup

❋

3 ripe tomatoes
olive oil or good vegetable oil, for cooking
2 large shallots, finely chopped
1 clove garlic, finely chopped
1 tablespoon tomato paste, optional
bouquet garni (see page 61)

1 Bring a pan of water to a boil. Meanwhile, cut a small cross in the bases of the tomatoes. Put them in a bowl, cover with boiling water and let stand for 10 seconds before plunging them into a bowl of iced water. Drain and, with the point of a sharp knife, remove the stalk and then peel, quarter and remove the seeds. Coarsely chop the flesh.
2 Heat a little oil in a skillet and add the shallots and garlic. Cook gently until softened, but not brown. Stir in the tomato paste if the fresh tomatoes are not particularly ripe.
3 Add the tomatoes to the pan with the bouquet garni and cook rapidly, stirring constantly with a wooden spoon, for about 7 minutes, or until the mixture is dry. Remove the bouquet garni and season to taste with salt and pepper.

Pesto (top) and Tomato concassé

Mango and cilantro salsa

This tropical salsa is delicious served with broiled scallops or fish kebabs as pictured.

Preparation time **15 minutes + 30 minutes chilling**
Total cooking time **None**
Makes approximately 1¹/₂ cups

3 ripe mangoes
2 scallions, finely chopped
¹/₄ cup chopped fresh cilantro
2 tablespoons lime juice, or to taste
finely chopped peeled fresh ginger root, to taste

1 Peel the skin from the mangoes, using a small paring knife. Slice down either side of the stone to release the flesh. Cut the flesh into evenly sized cubes and place in a small bowl.

2 Add the scallions and cilantro to the bowl and season with freshly ground black pepper. Stir to combine and add the lime juice and fresh ginger, to taste. Cover the bowl with plastic wrap and chill for 30 minutes before serving. Serve with cold meats, broiled fish or chicken dishes.

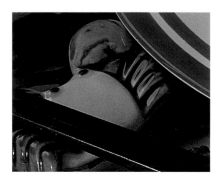

Sweet-and-sour sauce

This sauce, with a Chinese influence, goes extremely well with stir-fried shrimp, as shown here.

Preparation time **8 minutes**
Total cooking time **10 minutes**
Makes approximately **2/3 cup**

1 1/2 **teaspoons cornstarch**
1/4 **cup vinegar**
2 **tablespoons brown sugar**
1/4 **cup pineapple juice**
2 **tablespoons ketchup**
2 **teaspoons soy sauce**

1 Dissolve the cornstarch in 1 1/2 teaspoons water and set aside. Add the remaining ingredients to a small saucepan and bring to a boil.
2 When the mixture is boiling, lower the heat, whisk in the combined cornstarch and water and stir for about 5 minutes, or until thickened. Serve hot. This sauce goes well with deep-fried pork, stir-fried shrimp and chicken and can also be used as a dipping sauce for egg rolls.

Chinese lemon sauce

This is a classic Asian accompaniment for sautéed or deep-fried chicken strips. It also goes well with seafood and other poultry.

Preparation time **10 minutes**
Total cooking time **10 minutes**
Makes approximately **1 cup**

1/4 **cup lemon juice**
1/4 **cup chicken stock (see page 61)**
1 **tablespoon sugar**
1 **tablespoon honey**
1/2 **teaspoon grated peeled fresh ginger root**
1 **tablespoon cornstarch**
1–2 **drops yellow food coloring**

1 Put the lemon juice, stock, sugar, honey and ginger in a saucepan with 1/2 cup water. Stir over medium heat until the sugar dissolves.
2 Increase the heat and bring to a boil. Blend the cornstarch with a little water and add to the pan, stirring constantly until the sauce boils and thickens. Remove from the heat, stir in the food coloring and season with a pinch of salt. Serve immediately.

Sweet-and-sour sauce (top) and Chinese lemon sauce

Salsa roja

Salsas are on the table at every meal in Mexico. There are over 100 different types of chile and the hotness varies according to the particular chile, the soil and the climate. Tortilla corn chips are shown here with the salsa.

Preparation time **20 minutes + 2–3 hours refrigeration**
Total cooking time **None**
Makes approximately 3 cups

3 ripe tomatoes, seeded and chopped
I onion, chopped
3 serrano chiles, seeded and chopped
2 teaspoons salt
2 teaspoons lime juice
I tablespoon coarsely chopped fresh cilantro leaves

1 Stir all the ingredients in a bowl until well combined. Cover the bowl with plastic wrap and refrigerate for 2–3 hours to allow the flavors to mature.
2 You may serve this salsa chilled or at room temperature to accompany broiled fish, chicken, beef or as a dip with tortilla chips.

Chef's tips If you prefer a less chunky consistency, make the salsa in a food processor. Add the cilantro at the end after the salsa has been coarsely blended.

Serrano chiles are medium to hot in flavor.

Peanut dipping sauce

This popular and versatile dipping sauce can be served with a variety of saté sticks, such as the skewered chicken shown, or with vegetables, such as broccoli florets, carrot or bell pepper strips.

Preparation time **10 minutes**
Total cooking time **5 minutes**
Makes approximately 1¹/₄ cups

¹/₂ cup smooth peanut butter
I clove garlic, finely chopped, optional
¹/₄ cup canned unsweetened coconut milk
few drops of Tabasco, or to taste
I tablespoon honey
I tablespoon lemon juice
I tablespoon light soy sauce

1 Combine the peanut butter, garlic, coconut milk and ¼ cup water in a saucepan. Stir over medium heat for about 1–2 minutes, or until smooth and thick.
2 Add the Tabasco, honey, lemon juice and soy sauce and stir for about 1 minute, or until the sauce is warm and thoroughly combined.

Chef's tip Be careful not to overheat the sauce because it will separate easily.

Jus

A jus is gravy made from the sticky caramelized juices left in the pan after roasting veal, poultry, lamb or beef. We have shown it with lamb and steamed Asian greens.

*Preparation time **15 minutes***
*Total cooking time **30 minutes***
Makes approximately 1 cup

1 lb. roast of meat or poultry
2 cups brown stock for dark meats or
   chicken stock for lighter meats (see pages 60–61)
1 carrot, chopped
1 onion, chopped
1 stalk celery, chopped
1 leek, chopped
1 bay leaf
2 sprigs of fresh thyme
3 peppercorns

1 When the meat or poultry is cooked, remove it from the roasting pan and allow it to rest for 20 minutes. If there is a lot of fat in the pan, spoon off most of it, leaving enough to fry the vegetables. In a saucepan, heat the stock over medium heat.

2 Add the carrot, onion, celery and leek to the roasting pan and cook gently on top of the stove for 5 minutes, stirring constantly with a wooden spoon to prevent burning, until golden brown. Spoon off the excess fat from the pan and add the bay leaf, thyme and peppercorns. Stir in some of the hot stock, scraping the bottom of the pan with a wooden spoon constantly until it boils.

3 Pour in the remaining stock and bring to a boil. Reduce the heat to a simmer and cook for about 5–10 minutes, or until reduced by half, skimming the surface of foam or fat throughout cooking. Season to taste with salt and pepper and strain the jus into a gravy boat. Serve immediately.

Thickened pan gravy

This recipe can be made when roasting meats such as beef or chicken. It is shown with roast beef, Yorkshire pudding, potatoes and vegetables.

*Preparation time **15 minutes***
*Total cooking time **1–2 hours, depending on***
   meat chosen
Makes approximately 1¹/4 cups

oil, for cooking
meat or poultry of your choice, for roasting
¹/2 onion, cut into large cubes
1 small carrot, cut into large cubes
¹/2 stalk celery, cut into large pieces
2 cloves garlic, lightly crushed
1 bay leaf
2 sprigs of fresh thyme
¹/4 cup all-purpose flour
2 cups brown stock for dark meats or
   chicken stock for lighter meats (see pages 60–61)

1 Heat ¹/4 inch of oil in a roasting pan on top of the stove. Add the meat and turn and baste for about 5 minutes to seal all sides. Remove the meat from the pan. Add the vegetables, garlic and herbs to the pan. Place the meat over the vegetables and roast at the temperature appropriate for the meat.

2 When the meat is cooked, remove and keep it warm. Drain off any fat, leaving the juices and sediment behind with the vegetables. If necessary, add more color to the vegetables by frying them briefly on top of the stove in the roasting pan or returning to the oven to roast.

3 Stir in the flour and cook for 1 minute over low heat. Remove from the heat and slowly add the stock, stirring to prevent lumps from forming. Return to medium heat and stir until boiling. Lower the heat and simmer for 20 minutes, skimming froth and fat occasionally, then strain and season. Serve hot.

Jus (top) and Thickened pan gravy

Bordelaise sauce

A sauce from the Bordeaux region of France, traditionally made with wine, shallots and bone marrow. The bone marrow in this particular recipe, however, is optional, the sauce is also delicious without it. It is pictured here with grilled steak.

Preparation time **10 minutes**
Total cooking time **20 minutes**
Makes approximately 1 cup

**3/4 lb. beef marrow bone (shank), cut into
    4-inch lengths, optional**
4 shallots, very finely chopped
6 peppercorns
I sprig of fresh thyme
1/2 bay leaf
1 1/2 cups red wine
1 3/4 cups brown veal stock (see page 60)
I tablespoon unsalted butter, cut up and chilled

1 If using the marrow bone, prepare it by placing the pieces of bone in enough cold water to cover, then simmer for about 5 minutes, or until the marrow slips out easily. Thinly slice the marrow.
2 Place the shallots in a wide-bottomed saucepan with the peppercorns, thyme and bay leaf. Stir in the red wine and bring to a boil. Reduce by simmering briskly for about 3 minutes, or until the liquid has evaporated and the pan is almost dry.
3 Stir in the veal stock, scraping the bottom of the pan with a wooden spoon, and return to a boil. Reduce the heat and simmer for 10 minutes, or until the sauce is reduced to 1 cup. Skim the surface of the sauce occasionally. Season to taste with salt and pepper and skim the surface of the sauce again. Strain through a fine strainer before whisking in the butter, piece by piece, until the sauce has thickened slightly. Finish by adding the bone marrow, reheated by simmering in water or tossing in a hot skillet. Serve hot.

Shellfish sauce

With similar ingredients to those used in a bisque, this sauce is perfect with all types of shellfish, especially lobster as shown.

Preparation time **20 minutes**
Total cooking time **1 hour**
Makes approximately 1 1/3 cups

vegetable oil, for cooking
2 cloves garlic, lightly crushed
1/2 onion, coarsely diced
I small carrot, coarsely diced
I stalk celery, chopped
I bay leaf
2 sprigs of fresh thyme
**I lb. seafood shells such as crab, lobster
    or shrimp shells**
1/3 cup white wine
1/4 cup Cognac
1/4 cup all-purpose flour
2 tablespoons tomato paste
2 small tomatoes, stems removed, halved and seeded
I quart fish stock (see page 61)
1/4 cup heavy cream, optional

1 Heat the oil and garlic gently in a large deep saucepan. Add the vegetables and cook, stirring occasionally, until the vegetables are soft and have become lightly colored.
2 Stir in the bay leaf, thyme and shells. Pour in the wine and Cognac, scraping the base of the pan to lift all the juices. Cook until the pan is nearly dry. Sprinkle the flour in and stir in the tomato paste and tomatoes. Add the stock and stir until boiling. Reduce the heat and simmer for 30–40 minutes, stirring occasionally.
3 Strain into a clean saucepan and keep warm. Season with salt and pepper and add the cream, if using. Serve hot.

Bordelaise sauce (top) and Shellfish sauce

Mayonnaise

Mayonnaise can be used as a sauce or a salad dressing. It is shown here with hard-cooked eggs, pumpernickel, olives, capers and pickles. See page 62 for instructions to accompany this recipe.

Preparation time **10 minutes**
Total cooking time **None**
Makes approximately 1³/4 cups

2 egg yolks
3 tablespoons Dijon mustard, or 1 heaped
   teaspoon powdered mustard
ground white pepper, to taste
1–1¹/4 cups peanut or olive oil
1 tablespoon white wine vinegar

1 Bring all the ingredients to room temperature. Place a large deep bowl on a towel to prevent it from moving. Add the egg yolks, mustard, ground white pepper to taste, and 1 teaspoon salt, and mix well with a balloon whisk or with an electric mixer.
2 Put the oil in a measuring cup or anything from which it is easy to pour. While whisking or beating constantly, pour a thin stream of oil into the mixture. Begin with a small amount and stop beating periodically to allow each addition to emulsify to a thick, creamy mixture. Continue until ¹/3 cup of oil has been added.
3 The mayonnaise should have begun to thicken well at this stage. Add the vinegar. The texture will thin slightly. Continue to add enough of the remaining oil gradually until the mayonnaise reaches the desired consistency.
4 Adjust the flavor of the mayonnaise with a touch more vinegar or salt and whisk in 1–2 tablespoons of boiling water if it curdles or separates.
5 The mayonnaise can be stored for up to a week in the refrigerator. Use it as a base for a number of sauces, such as Thousand Island dressing and tartar sauce.

Thousand Island dressing

This creamy dressing is full of flavor and often served over a chef's salad. Shown here with salad leaves and shrimp, you could also use it in sandwiches or with burgers.

Preparation time **10 minutes + 20 minutes**
   refrigeration
Total cooking time **None**
Makes approximately 1¹/3 cups

1 cup homemade or good-quality
   commercial mayonnaise
¹/3 cup ketchup
¹/3 cup pepper relish or chili sauce
1 small onion, grated
1 red or green bell pepper, seeded and
   finely chopped
1 teaspoon Worcestershire sauce, or to taste
1 teaspoon Tabasco, or to taste
1 teaspoon brandy, or to taste

1 In a bowl, stir the mayonnaise, ketchup and pepper relish until combined. Stir in the onion, bell pepper, Worcestershire sauce, Tabasco and brandy, each to taste.
2 Cover the bowl with plastic wrap and refrigerate until needed. Make the dressing at least 20 minutes ahead of serving and keep covered in the refrigerator to allow the flavors to develop.

Chef's tip Try serving this dressing on a crisp salad of iceberg lettuce. To turn the salad into a meal, add chilled cooked shrimp and large garlicky croutons.

Mayonnaise (top) and Thousand Island dressing

Caesar salad dressing

Caesar salad is often thought of as an American dish, but was actually created by Caesar Cardini in Tijuana, Mexico in the 1920s.

Preparation time **10 minutes**
Total cooking time **None**
Makes approximately 1 cup

☼

3 small cloves garlic, crushed
2 egg yolks
1/4 cup olive oil
1 teaspoon Worcestershire sauce
1 tablespoon lemon juice
1/2 cup grated Parmesan

1 Using a balloon whisk or an electric mixer, whisk the crushed garlic and egg yolks together in a large glass bowl. Start adding the olive oil, drop-by-drop or in a thin stream, whisking constantly until the dressing starts to thicken.

2 Add the Worcestershire sauce. Continue whisking in the remaining oil, lemon juice and, finally, the grated Parmesan.

Chef's tip To make a Caesar salad, toss washed and dried salad leaves in a large bowl with the dressing. Remove the crusts from four slices of bread and cut into small cubes. Fry in 2 tablespoons olive oil until crisp and golden brown. Sprinkle the croutons over the salad, then top with several canned anchovy fillets and some grated Parmesan.

Sauce verte

This colorful, mayonnaise-based sauce complements dishes such as the poached salmon fillet shown here.

*Preparation time **20 minutes***
*Total cooking time **15 minutes***
Makes approximately 1¹/2 cups

❂

I cup firmly packed young spinach leaves
3 tablespoons fresh tarragon leaves
I teaspoon chopped fresh chives
3/4 cup chopped fresh chervil or parsley
1²/3 cups trimmed watercress leaves
I clove garlic, coarsely chopped
I cup homemade or good-quality
   commercial mayonnaise

1 Wash the spinach leaves thoroughly in cold water until all traces of sand or dirt are removed. Drain. Wash the herbs thoroughly and drain.
2 Combine all the greenery in a food processor with the garlic and 2 tablespoons water. Purée until fine.
3 Pour the mixture into a heavy-bottomed saucepan, heat gently to simmering and cook until the mixture appears to be dry and looks slightly separated. Strain immediately through a cheesecloth-lined strainer. Cool a little until you can bring the ends of the cheesecloth together and twist to squeeze out any remaining moisture. Discard the liquid.
4 In a bowl, combine a small amount of the mayonnaise with the dry purée to lighten it. Add to the remainder of the mayonnaise to make a bright green sauce. Taste and season. Serve cold with salads, cold poached poultry and fish, soups and terrines.

Marie Rose sauce

Adjust the flavorings in this sauce to your own taste and serve with your favorite seafood, such as the broiled scallops and shrimp pictured.

*Preparation time **5 minutes***
*Total cooking time **None***
Makes approximately 1¹/3 cups

❂

I cup homemade or good-quality
   commercial mayonnaise
¹/3 cup ketchup
Worcestershire sauce, to taste
Tabasco, to taste
brandy, to taste

1 Stir the mayonnaise and ketchup together in a small bowl. Add a few drops each of Worcestershire sauce, Tabasco and brandy and stir to combine.
2 Cover the sauce with plastic wrap and chill in the refrigerator. Serve with seafood.

Sauce verte (top) and Marie Rose sauce

Rémoulade sauce

This sauce is traditionally served with grated celery root, it is also delicious with cold meats such as the ham, turkey and pastrami shown here.

*Preparation time **10 minutes + 10 minutes**
   refrigeration + 15 minutes soaking
Total cooking time **None**
Makes approximately 1¹/4 cups*

☼

3 canned anchovy fillets
¹/4 cup milk
I cup homemade or good-quality
   commercial mayonnaise
2 teaspoons Dijon mustard
I tablespoon drained capers, chopped
3 tablespoons chopped dill or sweet pickles

1 Place the anchovy fillets in a small bowl, soak in the milk for 15 minutes, then drain. Discard the milk and finely chop the anchovies.
2 Stir the mayonnaise in a small bowl with the chopped anchovies and mustard until combined. Mix the capers and the pickles into the sauce.
3 Cover with plastic wrap and place in the refrigerator to chill for 10 minutes, or until required for serving. Serve the rémoulade sauce with broiled fish, shredded raw celery root or cold meats.

Classic vinaigrette

A classic vinaigrette may be used to add a tang to all types of salads or vegetables. Here it is shown simply with mixed salad leaves.

*Preparation time **5 minutes**
Total cooking time **None**
Makes approximately 1 cup*

☼

2 tablespoons Dijon mustard
3 tablespoons white wine vinegar
³/4 cup olive oil or good-quality salad oil

1 Whisk together the mustard and vinegar in a bowl, with salt and pepper to taste.
2 Slowly drizzle in the oil, whisking constantly. This will result in an emulsification, giving a thick smooth texture, rather than the oil separating and sitting on top. If the vinaigrette is too sharp for your taste, add a little more oil.
3 The vinaigrette may be kept at room temperature, in a sealed container and out of direct sunlight, for up to 1 week before serving.

Chef's tip As a rule of thumb, the guide for vinaigrettes is one part acid (wine vinegar or lemon juice) to four parts oil.

Rémoulade sauce (top) and Classic vinaigrette

Raspberry vinaigrette

*This delicious vinaigrette is shown served with
avocado and green salad leaves.*

Preparation time **10 minutes**
Total cooking time **None**
Makes approximately 1 cup

3/4 cup raspberries, fresh or frozen
3 tablespoons white wine vinegar
1 tablespoon sugar, or to taste
3/4 cup corn oil or good-quality salad oil

1 Process the raspberries and the vinegar in a blender
or food processor to a smooth purée. If the raspberries
are quite sharp or out of season, you may add the sugar
at this stage.
2 While the blender is still operating, gradually add the
oil in a thin stream. Season the vinaigrette to taste with
salt and pepper and then strain through a fine strainer
to remove the seeds. The vinaigrette can be served
immediately or covered and kept in the refrigerator for
up to 48 hours, though the color will be dulled a little
by storage.

Gribiche sauce

Particularly good to enliven mild foods.
Try serving this sauce with vegetables,
such as artichokes or white asparagus.

Preparation time **10 minutes**
Total cooking time **None**
Makes approximately 1 cup

1 cup vinaigrette (see page 44)
1/2 tablespoon chopped dill or sweet pickles
1/2 tablespoon chopped capers
1/2 tablespoon chopped scallions
1/2 hard-cooked egg, sieved

1 Stir the vinaigrette, pickles, capers, scallions and egg in a bowl until combined. Season to taste with salt and freshly ground black pepper.
2 You may serve the sauce immediately or cover with plastic wrap and refrigerate for up to 24 hours.

Chef's tips Strain the egg through a stainless metal strainer, a nylon strainer is too soft and you will find it difficult to push through.
    Serve with fish dishes such as poached trout or bass, or cooked artichoke bottoms or hearts.

Cucumber vinaigrette

An interesting variation on a classic vinaigrette.
Delicious served with smoked trout as pictured here.

Preparation time **15 minutes**
Total cooking time **5 minutes**
Makes approximately 1 cup

1/2 cucumber, about 3 oz.
1 tablespoon white wine vinegar
1 tablespoon Dijon mustard
1/3 cup light salad oil, such as
    corn or peanut

1 Heat a small saucepan of salted water to a boil. Peel the cucumber and reserve both the flesh and the peel. Remove and discard the cucumber seeds. Add the peel to the water, return to a boil and lower the heat to simmer until just tender. Drain the peel and place in a bowl of iced water for 10 seconds, then drain. Process the peel in a blender with the vinegar and mustard until it makes a smooth purée.
2 While the blender is running, gradually add the oil in a thin steady stream. Add the cucumber flesh and continue to a purée. Season with salt and pepper, to taste. Strain if a smoother texture is required. This vinaigrette may be refrigerated, covered with plastic wrap, for up to 2 days, but ideally should be served within 1–2 hours.

Gribiche sauce (top) and Cucumber vinaigrette

Citrus fruit vinaigrette

This dressing is well suited to being served with a salad to accompany goose, pork or Chinese barbecued duck as shown in the picture.

*Preparation time **15 minutes + 1–2 hours standing***
*Total cooking time **None***
Makes approximately 2 cups

juice and finely grated rind of 1 orange
juice and finely grated rind of 1 lemon
juice and finely grated rind of 1/2 grapefruit
1 1/4 cups corn oil or other good-quality
   salad oil

1 Place the rinds and fruit juices in a bowl. Gradually whisk the oil into the mixture and season to taste with salt and pepper. This can be done in a blender.
2 Cover with plastic wrap and let stand at room temperature for 1–2 hours to allow the flavors to mature before serving.

Chef's tip The quantity of oil may be decreased or increased depending on the size of the fruit and according to personal taste.

Vinaigrette à l'ancienne

This dressing derives its name from the coarse-grain mustard used, known as moutarde à l'ancienne *in French. It is shown here with a potato and chive salad.*

*Preparation time **5 minutes***
*Total cooking time **None***
Makes approximately 1 1/4 cups

1 tablespoon coarse-grain mustard
3 tablespoons white wine vinegar
3/4 cup good-quality salad oil

1 Place the mustard and vinegar in a bowl with salt and pepper to taste and whisk together.
2 Place the bowl on a towel to prevent it from moving while adding the oil. Gradually add the oil, pouring it in a thin steady stream, while whisking constantly. This will prevent the vinegar and oil separating.

Chef's tip The amount of oil used will alter the piquancy and thickness of the dressing. Less oil in the recipe will produce a sharper taste and thinner texture.

Citrus fruit vinaigrette (top) and Vinaigrette à l'ancienne

Blue cheese dressing

Very versatile, this all-time favorite dressing may be served with either vegetables, pears or avocado as shown here.

*Preparation time **15 minutes***
*Total cooking time **None***
Makes approximately 1¹/₃ cups

¹/₂ **cup crumbled blue cheese,**
   (Roquefort or Stilton are ideal)
¹/₃ **cup white wine vinegar**
²/₃ **cup light olive oil**
³/₄ **cup finely chopped fresh parsley**

1 In a small glass bowl, mash the blue cheese to a smooth paste with a fork.
2 To make a vinaigrette, in a separate bowl, whisk together the vinegar and salt and pepper to taste. While whisking, gradually add the oil in a thin steady stream until the mixture is thick and smooth.
3 Pour the vinaigrette over the cheese and add the chopped parsley. Stir the mixture until the dressing is smooth but retains some of the cheese chunks. Adjust the flavor with salt and pepper if necessary. Serve with avocado, pieces of fresh fruit or vegetables for dipping, and green salads.

Dill sauce

This slightly sweet sauce is the popular accompaniment to Scandinavian gravlax, as shown here, or any other smoked fish.

*Preparation time **10 minutes***
*Total cooking time **None***
Makes approximately ²/₃ cup

I heaped teaspoon coarse-grain mustard
I heaped tablespoon Dijon mustard
¹/₂ **teaspoon sugar**
¹/₃ **cup peanut oil**
I tablespoon white wine vinegar
I tablespoon chopped fresh dill weed

1 Place a large glass bowl on a folded towel to prevent it from moving. Whisk the coarse-grain mustard, Dijon, sugar and a pinch of salt in the bowl until well blended.
2 Pour the oil into the mixture in a very fine steady stream while whisking constantly. It is easier to pour the oil if you place it in a glass measuring cup. Continue until the mixture has thickened and approximately half the oil has been added. Slowly add all the vinegar while still whisking and finally, continue until all the oil has been added and the mixture has emulsified smoothly.
3 Stir in the chopped dill and add 1 tablespoon of hot water (this is a safety measure which helps to prevent the emulsified sauce from separating).

Blue cheese dressing (top) and Dill sauce

Chocolate sauce

A delightful accompaniment for many desserts and fruits, such as the poached pear and vanilla ice cream shown here.

Preparation time **10 minutes**
Total cooking time **20 minutes**
Makes approximately 1¹/4 cups

❀

3/4 cup sugar
2/3 cup chopped semisweet chocolate
1/4 cup good-quality unsweetened cocoa, sifted

1 Combine 1¹/4 cups of water with the sugar and chopped chocolate in a medium saucepan and slowly bring to a boil, stirring constantly. Remove from the heat.

2 In a bowl, mix the cocoa and 3 tablespoons water to a smooth paste. Pour this into the saucepan over medium heat and bring back to a boil, whisking vigorously and constantly. Simmer, uncovered, for 5–10 minutes, until the sauce coats the back of a spoon. Do not allow the sauce to boil over. Strain and allow to cool a little.

Chef's tip This sauce may be served hot or cold and keeps well for up to 1 week if stored in an airtight container in the refrigerator. To reheat, stir in the top of a double boiler, over hot water.

Butterscotch sauce

A very rich sauce ideal to serve hot with ice cream. It also works particularly well with waffles.

Preparation time **5 minutes**
Total cooking time **15 minutes**
Makes approximately 1¹/4 cups

❀ ❀

1 vanilla bean, split lengthwise
2 cups whipping cream
3/4 cup sugar

1 Scrape the seeds from the vanilla bean and add with the bean to a saucepan with the cream. Bring slowly to a boil, remove from the heat and allow the flavors to infuse into the cream, then strain and discard the vanilla bean.

2 In a separate heavy-bottomed saucepan and using a wooden spoon, stir half the sugar constantly over medium heat, until the sugar has melted. Add the remaining sugar and cook until the sugar is fluid and light golden.

3 Remove from the heat and add the cream in a slow steady stream, stirring constantly. Be careful as the sugar will splatter when the liquid is added. When all the cream has been incorporated, return to a boil and cook, stirring, until the sauce coats the back of the spoon. If you have a few lumps of sugar left in the bottom of the pan simply pass the liquid through a wire strainer. This sauce may be served either hot or cold.

Chef's tip For an adult version of the sauce, try adding a little malt whisky to taste. You could also add a little espresso coffee to taste.

Chocolate sauce (top) and Butterscotch sauce

Fruit coulis

Make this fabulous fruit sauce using any berries in season. Ideal for serving with any dessert, ice cream or sorbet.

Preparation time **5 minutes**
Total cooking time **5 minutes**
Makes approximately 1 cup

2 cups firm ripe raspberries
1/2 cup sugar
juice of 1/2 lemon
alcohol or liqueur of your choice

1 Prepare the fruit by picking over and removing any bruised or overripe fruit.
2 Combine the raspberries in a medium saucepan with the sugar and lemon juice and bring to a boil to soften the berries slightly. Remove from the heat and allow to cool.
3 Transfer to a food processor and blend to a smooth purée. Pass through a fine strainer to remove the seeds. At this stage your favorite alcohol can be added, to taste. This sauce can be kept in a covered container in the refrigerator for up to 1 week and should be served cold.

Chef's tips Try Kirsch, Calvados, eau de vie de poivre, or Cointreau.

When fresh berries are not available, use frozen ones instead. Thaw them before use. You may need to adjust the sugar content accordingly.

A quick, non-cook method if the fruit is very soft and will purée easily is to process with confectioners' sugar, strain and then add the lemon juice.

Orange and Grand Marnier sauce

Crêpes or ice cream can be dressed up with this sophisticated tangy sauce.

Preparation time **10–15 minutes**
Total cooking time **20 minutes**
Makes approximately 1 1/4 cups

1 cup fresh orange juice
2 tablespoons sugar
1 teaspoon finely grated orange rind
3/4 cup unsalted butter, cut into small cubes and chilled
1/4 cup Grand Marnier, Cognac or Cointreau

1 Bring the orange juice, sugar and orange rind slowly to a boil in a saucepan. Continue to boil, stirring occasionally, until the liquid becomes syrupy.
2 Whisk the butter into the boiling liquid, piece by piece, until a smooth consistency is obtained. Remove the pan from the heat and add the liqueur to taste. Serve the sauce immediately or keep it warm (not hot) for no more than about 30 minutes before use in the top of a double boiler over hot water.

Chef's tip If the sauce becomes too cold, it will set. If it is too hot, it will separate. To rescue the sauce from both problems, melt the former to a lukewarm heat and cool the latter to the same temperature. You can do this by bringing a small amount of water or orange juice to a boil, then whisking in a small amount of hard butter to obtain a smooth consistency. Slowly add either of the problem sauces to this mixture, whisking constantly.

White sauce

Flour and butter are cooked to make a roux to thicken white sauce.

Add the flour to melted butter in a saucepan over low heat. Stir with a wooden spoon.

Cook the flour mixture over the heat for 1–2 minutes, without browning, to create a roux.

Remove from the heat and gradually add the milk to the roux, beating until smooth.

Return to medium heat and bring to a boil, stirring constantly. Cook until the mixture thickens and coats the back of the spoon.

Mayonnaise

To make a successful mayonnaise, have all the ingredients at the same temperature.

Place a large, deep bowl on a towel to make it stable. Whisk the egg yolks, mustard, white pepper and salt in the bowl until evenly combined.

To begin with, whisk in a thin stream of oil until the mixture thickens. If the oil is added too quickly, the mayonnaise will separate.

After the first $1/3$ cup of oil has been added, whisk in the vinegar. Add the remaining oil gradually.

Hollandaise sauce

This sauce must not be allowed to get too hot, otherwise it may curdle.

Whisk the egg yolks and water together in a medium bowl or the top of a double boiler until foamy. Place the bowl or insert over a pan of hot water. Gradually whisk in the butter.

Continue adding the butter, whisking constantly. The sauce should leave a trail on the surface when the whisk is lifted.

Once all the butter is incorporated, strain the sauce into a clean bowl and then season to taste.

Clarifying butter

Removing the water and solids from butter makes it less likely to burn. Ghee is a form of clarified butter.

To make about $^1/_3$ cup clarified butter, cut $^3/_4$ cup butter into small cubes. Place in a small saucepan set into a larger pan of water over low heat. Melt the butter without stirring.

Remove the pan from the heat and allow to cool slightly. Skim the foam from the surface, being careful not to stir the butter.

Pour off the clear yellow liquid, being very careful to leave the milky sediment behind in the pan. Discard the sediment and store the clarified butter in an airtight container in the refrigerator.

Making crème anglaise

When making an egg custard sauce, keep the heat gentle and stir constantly to prevent scorching.

Stir the custard constantly over very low heat until the sauce thickens. Test the consistency by running your finger through the custard along the back of a wooden spoon. It should leave a clear line.

First published in the United States in 1998 by Periplus Editions (HK) Ltd., with editorial offices at
153 Milk Street, Boston, Massachusetts 02109.

Murdoch Books and Le Cordon Bleu thank the 32 masterchefs of all the Le Cordon Bleu Schools, whose knowledge and
expertise have made this book possible, especially: Chef Cliche (MOF), Chef Terrien, Chef Boucheret, Chef Duchêne (MOF),
Chef Guillut, Chef Steneck, Paris; Chef Males, Chef Walsh, Chef Hardy, London; Chef Chantefort, Chef Bertin, Chef Jambert,
Chef Honda, Tokyo; Chef Salembien, Chef Boutin, Chef Harris, Sydney; Chef Lawes, Adelaide; Chef Guiet, Chef Denis, Ottawa.
Of the many students who helped the Chefs test each recipe, a special mention to graduates David Welch and Allen Wertheim.
A very special acknowledgment to Directors Susan Eckstein, Great Britain, and Kathy Shaw, Paris, who have been responsible for
the coordination of the Le Cordon Bleu team throughout this series.

The Publisher and Le Cordon Bleu also wish to thank Carole Sweetnam for her help with this series.

First published in Australia in 1998 by Murdoch Books®

Managing Editor: Kay Halsey
Series Concept, Design and Art Direction: Juliet Cohen
Editor: Wendy Stephen
Food Director: Jody Vassallo
Food Editors: Dimitra Stais, Tracy Rutherford
US Editor: Linda Venturoni Wilson
Designer: Annette Fitzgerald
Photographers: Chris Jones, Jon Bader
Food Stylists: Mary Harris, Amanda Cooper
Food Preparation: Michelle Earl, Kerrie Mullins, Michelle Lawton
Chef's Techniques Photographer: Reg Morrison
Home Economists: Anna Beaumont, Michelle Earl, Michelle Lawton, Kerrie Mullins, Justine Poole, Kerrie Ray, Alison Turner

Library of Congress catalog card number: 98-65971
ISBN 962-593-430-8

Front cover: Crème anglaise

Distributed in the United States by
Charles E. Tuttle Co., Inc.
RR1 Box 231-5
North Clarendon, VT 05759
Tel: (802) 773-8930
Fax: (802) 773-6993

PRINTED IN SINGAPORE

05 04 03 02 01 00 99 98   10 9 8 7 6 5 4 3 2 1

Important: Some of the recipes in this book may include raw eggs, which can cause salmonella poisoning.
Those who might be at risk from this (the elderly, pregnant women, young children and those suffering
from immune deficiency diseases) should check with their physicians before eating raw eggs.